MASCOT
KIDS!

www.mascotbooks.com

Louisiana Dreams

For more information, please contact:
Mascot Books
620 Herndon Parkway, Suite 320
Herndon, VA 20170
info@mascotbooks.com

Library of Congress Control Number: 2021909895

CPSIA Code: PRT0821A
ISBN-13: 978-1-64543-990-5

Printed in the United States

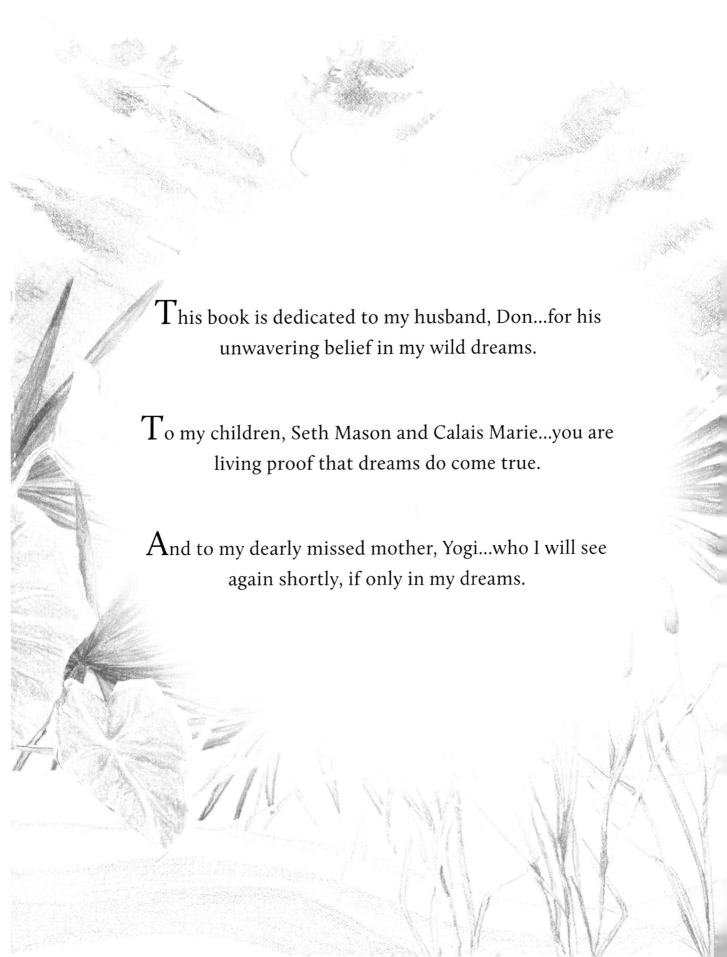

This book is dedicated to my husband, Don...for his unwavering belief in my wild dreams.

To my children, Seth Mason and Calais Marie...you are living proof that dreams do come true.

And to my dearly missed mother, Yogi...who I will see again shortly, if only in my dreams.

Go to sleep sweet child. Tomorrow will be another day.

Rest your eyes, my baby, again tomorrow you can play.

Va faire do-do mon cher bébé. Demain ça va être une autre journée.

Laissez tes yeux se reposer mon bien aimé, encore demain tu peux jouer.

Dream of wonderful and happy things, of your most favorite day...

Dream of your best memories, and live them out as you lay.

Fais des beaux rêves des jolis merveilles, de ta journée la plus préférée…

Rêve de tes plus beaux souvenirs et vis tout ça équand t'es couché.

Dream of conquering our waters, and of catching that uncatchable fish.

Dream of dark nights at warm bonfires, under bright stars to hang each wish.

Rêve de vaincre tous nous eaux, et d'attraper le poisson pas attrapable.

Rêve des nuits sombres aux feux de camp bien réchauffants en bas des étoiles qui brille pour pendre chaqu'un de tes souhaits.

Close your eyes and smell the sweet sugar cane that floats all around you here.

Know that you are a loved and lucky child, as this day begins to disappear.

Fremez tes yeux et sentir la douce canne-à-sucre qui flotte tout autour de toi.

Faut connaître que t'as d'la chance et que t'es bien aimé équand cette journée commence à se coucher.

In the land where your roots were planted.
In the soil that grew us all.

Near the beautiful bayou banks we
branched out, and up, and tall.

Dans cette terre ayoù tes racines sont plantées. Dans le sol qui nous a tous élevés.

Proche à des jolis bords de bayous, on s'est branché au large et en haut.

Dream of the crawfish boils, the festivals, the parades, and the fun!

Dance to the rhythms that surround you, the jazz, the zydeco, and the drum!

Rêve des bouillions d'écrevisses, des festivals, des parades, et tout l'agrément!

Danse aux rythmes tout autour de toi, le Jazz, le Zydeco, et le tambour!

Dream of your most loved meals, the gumbo, the etouffee', the sweets!

Eyes shut tight, as you enjoy each bite, a king cake, a beignet, such treats!

Rêve de tout tes plats préférées, le Gombo, les étouffées, les douceurs!

Frême bien tes yeux, en mangeant chaque bouchée, un gâteau de roi, un beignet, quel bonheur!

Think of all our animals, the gators, the birds, the wild things you have seen!

Send up thanks that they too live here, in our Louisiana, so rich, and sacred, and green.

Jongle à tous nos animaux, les cocodrils, les zoiseaux, et toutes les bêtes farouches que t'as vu.

Envoie des "merci"s en haut parce qu'eux -autres aussitte, ça habite icitte dans notre chère Louisiane si riche, si bénie, et si verte.

Let the soft melodic buzz of our swamps hold your gaze so tight.

Let the hiss and hum of possibilities become electric for you tonight!

Laisse le doux "buzz" mélodique de nos marais teindre ton regard si fort.

Laisse le "hiss" et le "hum" de toutes les possibilités devient électrique pour toi à soir.

This place, this culture, this unforgettable life; is yours and mine, so rare!

It's now our job to dream new dreams for our Louisiana to share.

Cette place, cette culture, cette vie pas oubliable; c'est à toi et à moi, et c'est bien rare!

Et asteur, c'est ta job de faire des nouveaux rêves; comme ça notre Louisiane peut partager tout ça.

So count your rich blessings, thick as homemade syrup cake!

And plan new dreams even now, as sweet slumber you will make.

Ça fait, compter tes bénédictions si riches, épaisse comme le gâteau-sirop!

Et planner tes nouveaux rêves, même drette asteur avec le doux sommeil que tu vas faire.

Safe and sound you'll stay, protected with the strength of cypress trees.

As you dare to discover new worlds, beneath the mysterious, moss draped eves.

Bien secure tu vas rester, gardé par la force des arbres de cyprès.

Comme tu oses à découvrir les nouveaux mondes, en bas des branches de mystère couverts de mousse espagnol.

Hush, now my baby...Your dreams are ready to be freed from their wakeful cage.

Let your head fill with colorful characters, who are now coming onto the stage!

Shh, Shh mon bébé…Tes rêves sont parés à se libérer de leur cage de conscience.

Laisse ta tête se remplir avec des caractères bien colorés, ça monte sur l'estrade asteur!

You are so very tired, I know, but you have so much left to do!

Don't let this night get away without living an adventure, or two!

T'es si bien fatigué, je connais, mais t'as toujours plein à faire!

Laisse pas cette nuit s'en voler sans faire au moins un aventure, ou deux!

You are a child in a magical land, and your family loves you so!

This place has given you a million memories to take with you as you go.

T'es un enfant dans une terre magique, et ta famille t'aime si tant!

Cette place t'as donné un million de souvenirs pour prendre avec toi sur le chemin.

About the Author

Rebecka Bihm Lester is a native of Arnaudville, Louisiana, and often draws inspiration from her unique childhood in Cajun Country. She is a graduate of Cecilia High School and attended Spring Hill College in Mobile, Alabama, where she studied Philosophy. Rebecka worked in Social Services and Child Welfare for seventeen years before publishing her first book. The author currently lives in the sleepy beach town of Perdido Key, Florida, with her husband, two children, and three dogs.

About the Illustrator

Virginia Fuselier Geotting is a south Louisiana native. She has had a lifelong love of the arts. Virginia attended the University of Louisiana at Lafayette, where she studied visual arts. The artist currently lives in Lafayette, Louisiana, with her husband and two children.

About the Translator

Valerie Broussard Boston, a devoted francolouisianaise, is a teacher and lifelong student, who now lives in Japan with her husband and three daughters, who often have Louisiana Dreams.